GW00708379

Angels

A Joyous Celebration

RUNNING PRESS

PHILADELPHIA · LONDON

A Running Press® Miniature Edition™
© 1999, 2013 by Running Press
All rights reserved under the Pan-American and
International Copyright Conventions
Printed in China

ISBN 978-0-7624-4984-2

Running Press Book Publishers
2300 Chestnut Street
Philadelphia, PA 19103-4371

Visit us on the web!
www.runningpress.com

Contents

Introduction

A world without angels would be
a world without hope. Angels appear in the earliest stories of our
existence—winged creatures that be-
long to a higher order than man.
Angels are depicted as messengers,
musicians, guardians, cupids, and
even warriors. The angel is a bridge

between heaven and earth, a human form with divine alterations—wings, halos, and golden auras. They are divine messengers with grace and archetypal beauty or robust youths with bow and arrow or harp and flute. Some of the greatest painters and sculptors in the history of art have dealt with the image if the angel. Each artist brought to his rendering a combination of the traditional image and a personal vision. The combination of the unique and the common has produced some of the world's finest works of art.

The Greeks and Romans saw the angel as an allegory for divine wisdom or powers. Statues and frescoes commemorating triumph almost always used a winged figure to represent victory. The winged cupid represented the duality of love; the lovely, playful cherub wielded a bow and arrow in order to pierce the heart of his intended.

With the rise of Christianity, angels became icons of divine perfection—they were beautiful, graceful, loyal servants who performed varied services for the Almighty. They began to inhabit religious paintings in increasing numbers and in prominent posi-

tions. By the early Renaissance, the angel had become a favorite subject in painting, immortalized in the sublime perfection of works by artist such as Botticelli and Raphael.

The art of the post-Renaissance began a slow return to the secular world and its scenes, but angels remained a lasting symbol of the presence of the divine in our earthly realm. Angels continue to inhabit the conscience of our culture. They are not only part of our religious world but also part of our popular literature, myth, and fantasy. Angels are a reminder to us all of our well-being and serve as inspirations and examples of grace, happiness, and harmony. The more materialistic our world becomes, the more we embrace the idea that angels watch over us and change our lives.

Looking Down Upon Us

The guardian angels of life sometimes fly so high as to be beyond our sight, but they are always looking down upon us.

—Jean Paul Richter (1763–1825)
French writer and humorist

16

O, beautiful rainbow, all woven of light! Heaven surely is open when thou dost appear and bending above thee the angels draw near, and sing "The rainbow—the rainbow; the smile of God is here!"

—**Sarah J. Hale (1790–1879)**
American writer and editor

17

Angels are in the heavens, I am sure, because there are deeds done by mortals that are difficult to explain by the mortal nature of man. The angels of self-sacrifice and everlasting devotion, of courage and tenderness—they must be fluttering about in the winds high above, sometimes taking on the face of man and his flesh.

—Dagobert D. Runes (1902–1982)

American writer

For God will deign
To visit oft the dwellings of
    just men
Delighted, and with frequent
    intercourse
Thither will send his winged
    messengers
On errands of supernatural grace.

—John Milton (1608–1674)
English poet

The angels . . . regard our safety, undertake our defense, direct our ways, and exercise a constant solicitude that no evil befall us.

—John Calvin (1509–1564)
French theologian and reformer

He shall give his angels charge over thee, to keep thee in all thy ways.

—Psalm 91:11
The Bible

I've heard that little infants
    converse by smiles and signs
With the guardian band of angels
    that round them shines,
Unseen by grosser senses;
    beloved one! dost thou
Smile so upon the heavenly
    friends, and commune with
    them now?

—Caroline Anne Southey (1786–1854)
English poet

I have seen angels by the sick
    one's pillow;
Their's was the soft·tone and the
    soundless tread,
Where smitten hearts were
    drooping like the willow,
They stood 'between the living
    and the dead.'

       —Unknown

Four angels to my bed,
Four angels round
my head,
One to watch and one
to pray
And two to rear my
soul away.

—Thomas Ady
17th-century English writer

25

Beside each man who's born
on earth
A guardian angel takes
his stand,
To guide him through
life's mysteries.

—Menander of Athens (c. 343–291 B.C.)
Greek playwright and poet

26

There are two angels, that attend unseen
    unseen
Each one of us, and in great books
    record
Our good and evil deeds. He who writes down
The good ones, after every action,
    closes
His volume, and ascends with it
    to God,

The other keeps his dreadful day-
    book open
Till sunset, that we may repent;
    which doing,
The record of the action fades
    away,
And leaves a line of white across
    the page.

—Henry Wadsworth Longfellow (1807–1882)
American poet

When tempted, invoke
your angel. He is more
eager to help you than you are
to be helped! Ignore the devil,
and do not be afraid of him.
He trembles and flees
at your guardian angel's sight.

—St. John Bosco (Giovanni Melchior)
(1845–1888)
Italian priest and writer

When children lay them down to sleep,
Two angels come, their watch to keep,
Cover them up, safely and warm,
Tenderly shield them from harm.
But when they wake at dawn of day,
The two bright angels go away,
Rest from their work of care and love
For God Himself keeps watch above.

—Unknown

*We should pray
to the angels,
for they are
given to
us as guardians.*

—St. Ambrose (c. 340–397)
Italian bishop

If there be for him
an angel, an intercessor,
one among a thousand,
to vouch for man's
uprightness, then
He is gracious.

—Job 33:23
The Bible

Then, in such hour of need
Of your fainting, dispirited race,
Ye, like angels appear,
Languor is not in your heart,
Weakness is not in your word,
Weariness is not on your brow.

—Matthew Arnold (1822–1888)
English poet and critic

But Man, proud man,

Dress'd in a little brief authority,

Most ignorant of what he's
   most assur'd,

His glassy elegance, like an
   angry ape,

Plays such fantastic tricks before
   high heaven

As makes the angels weep.

—William Shakespeare (1564–1616)
English playwright and poet

In this dim world of clouding cares,
We rarely know, till 'wildered eyes
See white wings lessening up the skies,
The angels with us unawares.

—Gerald Massey (1828–1907)
English poet

And with the morn,
   those angel faces smile
Which I have loved long
   since, and lost awhile.

—John Henry Newman (1801–1890)
English cardinal and theologian

Even the darkest soul passes, at least once in life, a ray of awareness of the supernatural, sometimes at the birth of a child or the death of a soul.

—Dagobert D. Runes (1902–1982)
American writer

If a man is called to be a streetsweeper, he should sweep streets even as Michelangelo painted, or Beethoven composed music, or Shakespeare wrote poetry. He should sweep streets so well that all the host of heaven and earth will pause to say, here lived a great streetsweeper who did his job well.

—Martin Luther King, Jr. (1926–1968)
American civil rights leader and minister

Every breath of air and ray
of light and heat,
every beautiful prospect,
is, as it were, the skirts
of their garments,
the waving of the robes of
those whose faces see God.

—John Henry Newman (1801–1890)
English cardinal and theologian

42

He passed the flaming bounds of place
and time:
The living throne, the sapphire-blaze,
Where angels tremble, while they gaze,
He saw; but blasted with excess
of light,
Closed his eyes in endless night.

—Thomas Gray (1716–1771)
English poet

Angels . . . with beautiful wings of silk
and crowns of baby rosebuds . . . all
live together in a castle . . . and when the
angels want to go someplace they just
whistle—and a cloud floats to the castle
door and picks them up. And the angels
ride through the sky riding the cloud
like a magic carpet—under the moon
and through the stars—until they're
right above us. That's how they can look
down and see if we're all right—and
sometimes even send messages to us.

—From the movie *The Little Princess*

Love and Compassion

Unless you can love,
  as the angels may,
With the breath of
  heaven betwixt you ...
Oh, never call it loving!

—Elizabeth Barrett Browning (1806–1861)
English poet

Love's heralds should be thoughts
Which ten times faster glide than
     the sun's beams
Driving back shadows over
     low'ring hills;
Therefore do nimble-pinion'd
     doves draw love;
And therefore hath the wind-swift
     Cupid wings.

—William Shakespeare (1564–1616)
English playwright and poet

49

Her beautiful hair
dropped over me—
like an angel's wing.

—Charles Dickens (1812–1870)
English writer

Love

I imagine the leathery sound of
wings—not bats but angels
lighting down, naked, gorgeous.

—Robert Ferro (1941–1988)
American writer

O Lyric love,
Half angel and half bird,
And all a wonder
And a wild desire.

—Robert Browning (1812–1889)
English poet

Stone walls do not a prison make
Nor iron bars a cage;
Minds innocent and quiet take
That for a hermitage;
If I have freedom in my love,
And in soul am free,
Angels alone that soar above
Enjoy such liberty.

—Richard Lovelace (1618–1657)
English poet

Self is the only prison that can
   ever find the soul;
Love is the only angel who can bid
   the gates unroll;
And when he comes to call thee,
   arise and follow fast;
His way may lie through darkness,
   but it leads to light at last.

—Henry Van Dyke (1822–1891)
American cleric and writer

Angels

Angels listen when she speaks:
She's my delight, all mankind's
wonder . . .

—John Wilmot Rochester (1647–1680)
English poet

I feel as if it would be flattering
an angel to compare such
a creature to you. You have
been privileged to receive
every gift from nature, you
have both fortitude and tears.

—Victor Hugo (1802–1885)
French writer

When love speaks, the voice
of all the gods
Makes heaven drowsy with
the harmony.

—William Shakespeare (1564–1616)
English playwright and poet

She was a phantom of delight
When first she gleamed upon
    my sight;
A lovely apparition . . .
And yet a spirit still and bright,
With something of an angel light.

—William Wordsworth (1770–1850)
English poet

. . . he fell asleep, and dreamed
he saw her coming bounding
towards him, just as she used to
come, with a wreath of
jessamine in her hair, her cheeks
bright, and her eyes radiant
with delight; but, as he looked,
she seemed to rise from
the ground; her cheeks wore a

paler hue—her eyes had a deep,
divine radiance, a golden halo
seemed around her head—
and she vanished from his sight . . .

—Harriet Beecher Stowe (1811–1896)
American writer

Of all earthly music
that which reaches farthest
into heaven is the beating
of a truly loving heart.

—Henry Ward Beecher (1813-1887)
American cleric

There is music even in the beauty, and the silent note which Cupid strikes, far sweeter than the sound of an instrument.

—Thomas Browne (1605–1682)
English physician and writer

Every saint in heaven is as a flower in the garden of God, and holy love is the fragrance and sweet odor that they all send forth, and with which they fill the bowers of that paradise above. Every soul there is, is a note in some concert of delightful music, that sweetly harmonizes with every other note, and all together blend in the most rapturous strains . . .

—Jonathan Edwards (1703–1758)
American cleric and theologian

O welcome, pure-ey'd Faith,

white-handed Hope,

Thou hovering angel,

girt with golden wings!

—John Milton (1608–1674)

English poet

For compassion a
human heart suffices;
but for full and adequate
sympathy with joy an
angel's only.

—Samuel Taylor Coleridge (1772–1834)
English poet and critic

Divine things must be loved to be known.

—Blaise Pascal (1623–1662)

French scientist and philosopher

Bearers of Music

Music

Music is well said to be
the speech of angels:
in fact, nothing among the
utterances allowed to man
is felt to be so divine. It
brings us near to the infinite.

—Thomas Carlyle (1795–1881)
Scottish writer and historian

Music soothes us, stirs us up;
it puts noble feelings in us;
it melts us to tears, we know not
how—it is a language by itself,
just as perfect, in its way,
as speech, as words;
just as divine, just as blessed . . .

—Charles Kingsley (1819–1875)
English cleric and writer

I want to be an angel,
And with the angels stand,
A crown upon my forehead,
A harp within my hand.

—Urania Bailey (1820–1882)
American evangelist and writer

In Heaven a spirit doth dwell
Whose heart-strings are a lute—
None sing so wild—so well
As the angel Israfel—
And the giddy stars are mute.

—Edgar Allan Poe (1809–1849)
American writer and poet

Where the bright seraphim
in burning row
Their loud up-lifted angel
trumpets blow.

—John Milton (1608–1674)
English poet

Let but the voice engender
the string,
And angels will be borne,
while thou dost sing.

—Robert Herrick (1591–1674)
English poet

The angels were all
    singing out of tune,
And hoarse with having
    little else to do,
Excepting to wind up
    the sun and moon
Or curb a runaway
    young star or two.

—George Gordon, Lord Byron (1788–1824)
English poet

84

Whether the angels play only
Bach in praising God I am not
quite sure; I am sure however,
that *en famille* they play Mozart.

—Karl Barth (1886–1968)
Swiss theologian and educator

So is music an asylum.
It takes us out of the actual
and whispers to us dim secrets
that startle our wonder as
to who we are, and for what,
whence and whereto.
All the great interrogatories,
like questioning angels,
float in on its waves of sound.

—Ralph Waldo Emerson (1803–1882)
American writer and poet

O may I join the choir
invisible of those immortal
dead who live again in
minds made better by their
presence: live in pulses
stirred to generosity, in
deeds of daring rectitude,
in scorn for miserable aims
that end with self,
in thoughts sublime that

§§

pierce the night like stars,
and with their mild
persistence urge man's
search to vaster issues.
So to live is heaven;
to make the undying
music in the world!

—George Eliot (Mary Ann Evans)
(1819–1880)
English writer

. . . Look how the floor of heaven

Is thick inlaid with patinas of bright
gold:

There's not the smallest orb which
thou behold'st

But in his motion like an angel sings,

Still quiring to the young-ey'd
cherubins;

Such harmony is in immortal souls . . .

—William Shakespeare (1564–1616)
English playwright and poet

Heaven and Earth

The world has
angels all too few,
And heaven is over-
flowing.

—Samuel Taylor Coleridge (1772–1834)
English poet and critic

If God could make angels, why did he bother with men?

—Dagobert D. Runes (1902–1982)
American writer

On the second day, God created
the angels, with their natural
propensity to good. Later
He made beasts with their animal
desires. But God was pleased
with neither. So He fashioned
man, a combination of angel and
beast, free to follow good or evil.

—Midrash Semak
Hebrew biblical text

The Earth is to the Sun

What man is to the angels.

—Victor Hugo (1802–1885)
French writer

There is a spiritual life that we
share with the angels of Heaven
and with the divine spirits, for like
them we have been formed
in the image and likeness of God.

—Lawrence of Brindisi (1559–1619)
Italian religious leader and writer

One of the hardest lessons we
have to learn in this life . . . is to
see the divine, the celestial,
the pure in the common, the near
at hand——to see that heaven lies
about us here in this world.

—John Burroughs (1837–1921)
American writer and naturalist

In pride, in reas'ning pride,
        our error lies;
All quit their sphere, and rush into
        the skies!
Pride still is aiming at the bless'd
        abodes,
Men would be Angels,
Angels would be Gods.
Aspiring to be Gods, the Angels fell,
Apsiring to be Angels men rebel.

—Alexander Pope (1688–1744)
English poet

How fading are the joys we dote
  upon!
Like apparitions seen and gone.
But those which soonest take
  their flight
Are the exquisite and strong—
Like angels' visits, short and bright;
Mortality's too weak to bear them
  long.

—John Norris (1657–1711)

English philosopher and cleric

Millions of spiritual creatures

walk the earth

Unseen, both when we wake

and when we sleep.

—John Milton (1608–1674)
English poet

Much on earth is hidden
from us, but to make up
for that we have been given
a precious mystic sense
of our living bond with the …
higher heavenly world.

—**Fyodor Dostoyevsky (1821–1881)**
Russian writer

The only things we are missing
are angels. In this vast world
there is no place for them.
And anyway, would our eyes
recognize them? Perhaps
we are surrounded by angels
without knowing it.

—Henry Miller (1891–1980)
American writer

We only live among men, but there are airy hosts, blessed spectators, sympathetic lookers-on, that see and know and appreciate our thoughts and feelings and acts.

—Henry Ward Beecher (1813–1887)
American cleric

Outside the open window
The morning air is all awash
with angels.

—Richard Purdy Wilbur (b. 1921)
American poet

Outside the doors of study . . . an angel waits.

—Hannah Green
American writer

Be not forgetful to
entertain strangers,
for thereby some
have entertained
angels unawares.

—Hebrews 13:2
The Bible

If some people really
see angels where others see
only empty space,
let them paint the angels . . .

—John Ruskin (1819–1900)
English critic and writer

If angels are
entertained unaware,
it is because
they have tact.

—Spencer Bayne (1899–1978)
American writer

I should like to have had an
angelic brush, or forms of paradise
to fashion the archangel,
and to see him in Heaven, but I
have not been able to rise so high,
and in vain I have searched for him
on earth. So that I have looked
upon that form which I have
established for myself in the Idea.

—**Guido Reni (1575–1642)**
Italian artist

I have been on
the verge of being
an angel all my life,
but it's never
happened yet.

—Mark Twain (1835–1910)

American writer

The last thing I should expect to meet in heaven would be a dead level of intellect and taste. I admire the notion of some of the theologians that each individual angel is a distinct species in himself.

—Joseph Farrell
American academic and writer

Every man contemplates an angel in his future self.

—Ralph Waldo Emerson (1803–1882)
American writer and poet

An angel can illumine the thought and mind of man by strengthening the power of vision, and by bringing within his reach some truth which the angel himself contemplates.

—St. Thomas Aquinas (c. 1225–1274)
Sicilian-born Dominican theologian

The more materialistic science becomes, the more angels shall I paint: their wings are my protest in favor of the immortality of the soul.

—Edward Coley Burne-Jones (1833–1889)
English artist and designer

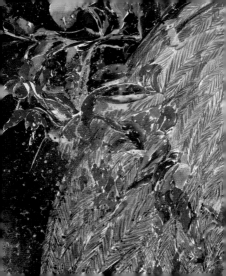

pp. 14–15: *Angel's descent*, detail, by Michael Chase.
Private Collection/The Bridgeman Art Library

p. 20: *Jose Maria y su Angel*, detail, by Cristina Rodriguez.
Private Collection/The Bridgeman Art Library

p. 27: *Elijah Visited by an Angel*, detail from the altarpiece
of the *Last Supper*, by Dirck Bouts. St. Peter's, Louvain,
Belgium/Giraudon/The Bridgeman Art Library

p. 32: Vault of Angels, detail of fresco. Santa Maria Church,
Arles-sur-Tech, France. ©Peter Willi/SuperStock

p. 38: *The Winged Robe Legend Higaromo*, detail, by
Liz Wright. Private Collection/The Bridgeman Art Library

pp. 46–47: *Cupid delivering Psyche*, detail, by Sir Edward
Burne-Jones. Private Collection/by courtesy of Julian
Hartnoll/The Bridgeman Art Library

p. 50: *Birth of Venus*, detail, by William-Adolphe Bouguereau.
Scala/Art Resource, NY

pp. 54–55: *Spirit from the Past*, detail, by Suad Al-Attar.
Private Collection/The Bridgeman Art Library

p. 58: *The Inspiration*, detail, by Gustave Moreau. Private Collection/Photo ©Christie's Images/The Bridgeman Art Library

p. 62: *Annunciatory Angel*, detail, by Fra Angelico. Detroit Institute of Arts, USA/Bequest of Eleanor Clay Ford/The Bridgeman Art Library

p. 67: *Angel Musician*, detail, by Melozzo da Forlì. Vatican Museums and Galleries, Vatican City, Italy/Giraudon/The Bridgeman Art Library

p. 70: *Putto* by Italian School. Kingston Lacy, Dorset, UK/National Trust Photographic Library/Derrick E. Witty/The Bridgeman Art Library

pp. 74–75: *The Concert of Angels*, detail, by Gaudenzio Ferrari. Sanctuary of Santa Maria delle Grazie, Saronno, Italy/The Bridgeman Art Library

p. 79: Ceiling fresco, detail, Rome, Italy. ©Corinda Cook

p. 82: *Trinity with Saints Ursula and Margaret*, detail, by Antonio Maria Viani. Palazzo Ducale, Mantua, Italy. ©SuperStock

p. 87: *The Last Judgment*, detail of stained glass, by French

This book has been bound
using handcraft methods and
Smyth-sewn to ensure durability.

The dust jacket and interior were
designed by Corinda Cook.

The photographs and illustrations
were researched by Susan Oyama.

The text was compiled by
Lauren Mucciolo.

The text was set in Caslon,
BeLucian, Gill Sans, Grimshaw
Script, and Franklin Gothic.